MATCH ★★★★★ ATTAX

WORLD TEAMS & PLAYERS

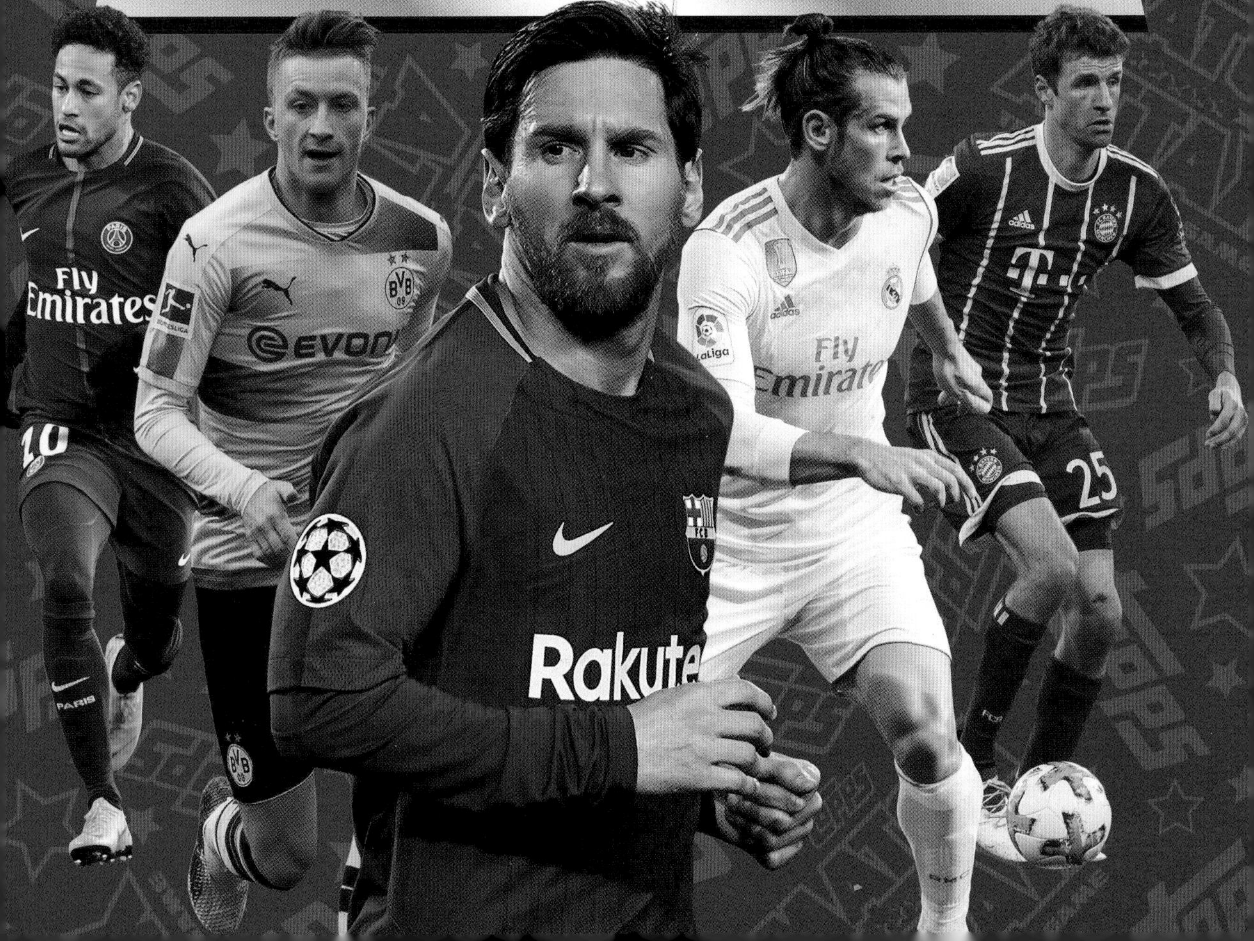

MY WORLD TEAMS & PLAYERS BOOK!

Epic clubs, global superstars, Champions League heroes, goal-crazy strikers... your World Teams & Players book has got the lot! Discover amazing stats, facts and stories about top teams like Barcelona, Real Madrid, Bayern Munich, Paris Saint-Germain and loads more.

MY NAME: ....

AGE: ....

CITY/TOWN: ....

MY THREE TOP TEAMS IN THE WORLD:

1 ....

2 ....

3 ....

MY THREE FAVE COUNTRIES:

1 ....

2 ....

3 ....

FAVE LA LIGA PLAYER: ....

....

FAVE BUNDESLIGA PLAYER: ....

....

It's me, the one and only, Ronaldo!

FAVE CHAMPIONS LEAGUE PLAYER:..
....

BUNDESLIGA WINNERS WILL BE:..
....

LA LIGA WINNERS:..
....

CHAMPIONS LEAGUE WINNERS WILL BE..
....

THE BEST FIFA MEN'S PLAYER WILL BE:..
....

Discover stacks of facts about the world's greatest players and footy legends from the past. Make sure you tackle the top quizzes and puzzles, too!

ON THE MAP!

Check out the biggest leagues and the greatest clubs from all around Europe!

A geography lesson? Get in!

Double homework for me please, teacher!

LA LIGA SPAIN

TEAMS: 20
STARTED: 1929

One of the most exciting leagues in the world! Barcelona and Real Madrid are the biggest clubs, with Atletico Madrid, Sevilla, Valencia and Villarreal also battling for glory.

PRIMEIRA LIGA PORTUGAL

TEAMS: 18
STARTED: 1934

Watch out for the top trio of Porto, Benfica and Sporting Lisbon scrapping it out for Portugal's Primeira Liga trophy! These three clubs have won every title since 2001, when Boavista were champions.

Bayern Munich won the European Cup three times in a row between **1974** and **1976**

LIGUE 1 FRANCE

TEAMS: 20
STARTED: 1932

In recent years, France's Ligue 1 has been transformed into an epic league to watch. Paris Saint-Germain, Monaco, Marseille and Lyon are the big clubs chasing the title!

EREDIVISIE NETHERLANDS

TEAMS: 18
STARTED: 1956

In their orange kit, the Netherlands national team is well-known around the world. The Eredivisie league is also packed with top talent and teams like Ajax, PSV and Feyenoord.

BUNDESLIGA GERMANY

TEAMS: 18
STARTED: 1963

Bayern Munich, Borussia Dortmund and FC Schalke are just some of Germany's mega clubs. Stars like Robert Lewandowski and Timo Werner bash in great goals every week!

SERIE A ITALY

TEAMS: 20
STARTED: 1898

Famous clubs like Juventus, AC Milan and Inter Milan bring glitz, glamour and goals to Italy's top league! Some of the world's most amazing players have starred in Serie A.

MORE EPIC LEAGUES: Jupiler Pro League **(BELGIUM)** • Premier League **(RUSSIA)** • Primera Division **(ARGENTINA)** • Superleague **(GREECE)** • Bundesliga **(AUSTRIA)** • Super Lig **(TURKEY)** • MLS **(USA & CANADA)** • Brasileirao **(BRAZIL)**

ALL ABOUT BARCELONA

Superstar Spanish club Barcelona is packed with talent, trophies and top new signings every year! Discover more about Barca's amazing story and success...

BRILL BARCA!

You could fill a book with the victories, epic players and fantastic history of Barcelona! This skilful Spanish team have been the most eye-catching club this century and had some of the best players on the planet. Footy legends like Andres Iniesta, Gerard Pique and Lionel Messi came through the club's famous youth system and heroes such as Luis Suarez and Ousmane Dembele arrived in mega transfers.

TROPHY TALK

It's a good job the Camp Nou stadium is so huge, because Barca need a massive place to show off all their trophies! Up to 2017, the club had picked up 24 La Liga titles, five Champions League, three FIFA Club World Cups, 29 Copa del Rey and 12 more top Euro honours. If there was a prize for Coolest World Club, they'd walk off with that one too!

STARS TO WATCH...

LUIS SUAREZ
STRIKER
Powerful shots & top tricks

PAULINHO
MIDFIELDER
Goalscoring central midfielder

OUSMANE DEMBELE
WINGER
Dribble & speed king

GERARD PIQUE
DEFENDER
Strong & clever on the ball

NICKNAME: Barca
STADIUM: Camp Nou
CAPACITY: 99,354
HOME KIT: Blue and red
YEAR FOUNDED: 1899
CLUB LEGENDS: Joan Gamper, Johan Cruyff, Lionel Messi, Xavi Hernandez, Pep Guardiola

Smile for the camera!

MAGIC MESSI

By March 2018, Messi had blasted an unbelievable 541 goals in just 625 Barcelona games! Since scoring his first in 2005 aged 17, he's the club's all-time top scorer and has won over 30 trophies in Spain. Messi is probably the most exciting player ever – he can dribble, trick or speed past defenders and creates goals and chances from nothing. The Argentine ace really is a little wizard with a magical left foot!

In the 2011–12 season, Argentine goal machine **Messi** scored 73 goals for **Barcelona** in all competitions.

CAPTAIN: Andres Iniesta **BIG BUY:** Philippe Coutinho (£142M in 2018) **YOUNG STAR:** Oriol Busquets

ALL ABOUT REAL MADRID

Goals, superstars, trophies and top transfers – Real Madrid fans always have plenty to cheer about at the Bernabeu!

GAME PLAN

Although much of Real's attacking play is built around their star striker Cristiano Ronaldo, the team is packed with goalscoring talent. Gareth Bale and Karim Benzema have over 250 club strikes between them and midfielders Marco Asensio, Isco, Luka Modric and Toni Kroos set up stacks of chances. Rock-hard defender Sergio Ramos also loves to hit the net!

TROPHY TALK

Champions League, La Liga, FIFA Club World Cup, UEFA Super Cup trophies... Real Madrid have lifted them all this decade! The Whites won 33 league titles between 1932 and 2017 and became the first club to win consecutive Champions League titles in 2016 and 2017. That year they won Europe's top prize for a record 12th time.

STARS TO WATCH...

MARCO ASENSIO
MIDFIELDER
Creative passer

RAPHAEL VARANE
DEFENDER
Perfect tackler

ISCO
MIDFIELDER
Trickster with ace shooting

GARETH BALE
FORWARD
Skilful left foot

CRISTIANO RONALDO

NICKNAME: The Whites
STADIUM: Bernabeu Stadium
CAPACITY: 81,044
HOME KIT: White
YEAR FOUNDED: 1902
CLUB LEGENDS: Raul, Alfredo Di Stefano, Ferenc Puskas, Zinedine Zidane, Cristiano Ronaldo

Cristiano Ronaldo has won the famous Ballon d'Or trophy **five times** – a joint record he shares with rival Lionel Messi.

Real Madrid paid **£80 million** to buy Ronaldo from Manchester United in **2009** – a world-record at the time.

The Portugal striker bagged his **324th** Real Madrid goal in **2015** to become the club's all-time top marksman.

His third Champions League title with the club in **2017** was his fourth overall. Cristiano also won it with Manchester United in **2008**.

Ronaldo notched up his **33rd** hat-trick in La Liga in **2018** with three strikes in a **5–2** win over Real Sociedad.

In February **2018** he scored his **100th** Champions League goal for Real Madrid.

In the same month, Ronaldo also reached **300** La Liga goals in just **285** games. That took his overall club total to 435!

Cristiano Ronaldo took over Real Madrid's famous No.7 shirt when Raul left the club in **2010**. In his first season he had No.9.

CAPTAIN: Sergio Ramos **BIG BUY:** Gareth Bale (£85m in 2013) **YOUNG STAR:** Oscar

ALL ABOUT

ATLETICO MADRID

Barcelona and Real Madrid need to watch out – Atletico Madrid are shooting for Spanish glory! It's time to reveal just how talented the team is...

SLICK STADIUM

Atletico moved into their amazing new stadium, the Wanda Metropolitano, at the start of the 2017–18 season. Before that they played at the Estadio Vicente Calderon for over 50 years. Their new ground holds approximately 68,000 fans, allows spectators to be closer to the pitch and has over 800 large TV screens. It will also host the 2019 Champions League final!

TROPHY TALK

Awesome Atletico Madrid are the third most successful club in La Liga, after Real Madrid and Barcelona. Between 1940 and 2014 they lifted ten championships and secured ten Copa del Rey wins. Legendary manager Diego Simeone is the man behind their recent success, but they lost the 2014 and 2016 Champions League finals to fierce city rivals Real Madrid.

STARS TO WATCH...

DIEGO GODIN
DEFENDER
Amazing heading skills

KOKE
MIDFIELDER
Bosses games with ease

ANTOINE GRIEZMANN
STRIKER
Pure goal machine

SAUL NIGUEZ
MIDFIELDER
Creative & energetic

NICKNAME: The Mattressers
STADIUM: Wanda Metropolitano
CAPACITY: 68,000
HOME KIT: Red and white
YEAR FOUNDED: 1903
CLUB LEGENDS: Diego Simeone, Fernando Torres, Luis Aragones, Adelardo, Sergio Aguero

GOAL GETTERS

Although Diego Simeone has turned Atletico Madrid into a very tough team to beat with powerful defenders, they also have some of the best attacking talent in Spain! Antoine Griezmann, Diego Costa and Kevin Gameiro fire in the goals in the league and Europe. Sergio Aguero, Radamel Falcao and Diego Forlan have all smashed the net for Atletico in the 21st century!

France star **Griezmann** scored his 100th goal for the club in February 2018. His first was in September 2014.

CAPTAIN: Diego Godin **TOP SCORER:** Luis Aragones (173) **BIG BUY:** Diego Costa (£57m in 2017)

ALL ABOUT VALENCIA

On the sunny east coast of Spain, Valencia's bright talents hope to take the club back to their La Liga and European glory days!

GAME PLAN

In the 2017–18 season, Valencia boss Marcelino kept the team in the chase for a top four Champions League spot in La Liga. Battling with Real Madrid, Sevilla and Villarreal, Valencia played with a counter-attacking style that saw them win 15 of their first 26 league games – an identical record to Real Madrid. Usually set up in a 4-4-2 formation, the first-choice strike pair of Simone Zaza and Rodrigo work hard to pressure the opposition and move Valencia forward.

TROPHY TALK

You have to go back to 2008 for Valencia's last major honour, when Juan Mata and David Villa helped them to the Copa del Rey. But, at the start of this century, Valencia were one of the top teams in Europe. Under manager Rafael Benitez they were La Liga champs in 2002 and 2004 and took the UEFA Cup and European Super Cup around that time, too.

STARS TO WATCH...

FRANCIS COQUELIN
MIDFIELDER
Plays anywhere in midfield

SANTI MINA
STRIKER
Exciting young goalscorer

GABRIEL PAULISTA
DEFENDER
Top tackling

NETO
GOALKEEPER
Strong in the box

NICKNAME: Los Che
STADIUM: Mestalla
CAPACITY: 55,000
HOME KIT: White and black
YEAR FOUNDED: 1919
CLUB LEGENDS: Mario Kempes, Rafael Benitez, David Villa, Edmundo Suarez, Fernando

PLAYER POWER

The backbone of Valencia in 2017–18 was Neto in goal, Ezequiel Garay in defence, Daniel Parejo and Geoffrey Kondogbia controlling midfield and Zaza snapping in attack. Francis Coquelin was signed from Arsenal to boost the middle of the pitch, with Goncalo Guedes and Carlos Soler defending and running down the wings. Valencia created a top team work-rate to take on the bigger Spanish teams!

Nice one – my kit matches the ball!

CAPTAIN: Daniel Parejo **TOP SCORER:** Edmundo Suarez (269) **YOUNG STAR:** Ferran Torres

LOOKIN' FOR LEGENDS!

These La Liga stars were red-hot in 2018! Can you find them all in the grid?

H	I	Q	O	S	D	M	V	O	L	J	Z	L	B	M	R
I	T	C	B	Z	T	A	T	U	D	O	Z	J	H	E	N
D	I	F	L	E	N	R	L	B	N	L	Q	Y	D	O	L
N	T	H	A	G	G	T	Y	Z	A	I	A	D	T	C	B
E	M	R	K	W	R	I	I	A	K	C	E	N	A	S	A
M	U	Z	W	W	A	N	O	R	D	Y	C	B	O	I	R
A	O	G	U	E	D	E	S	A	N	I	U	A	L	R	M
R	X	A	S	Y	B	Z	E	E	R	S	C	Q	S	M	K
R	S	Q	M	R	L	V	B	T	Q	J	S	D	U	B	A
A	R	B	X	A	J	C	M	U	S	T	S	I	Q	R	S
L	U	P	U	G	B	P	E	S	A	P	S	A	U	X	N
L	M	T	A	K	K	T	S	B	N	U	G	Q	Y	L	I
I	O	H	J	U	S	I	S	H	Z	D	Z	H	A	H	A
A	M	D	U	X	L	P	I	E	Y	E	P	I	N	H	Z
F	G	O	F	R	J	I	R	T	F	N	Z	O	N	Z	I
G	R	I	E	Z	M	A	N	N	H	S	Y	C	S	N	I
U	L	H	K	T	U	G	A	H	O	I	S	N	E	S	A
C	A	S	D	S	L	F	K	I	O	F	B	W	H	O	R

In **2017**, keeper **Jan Oblak** kept **3** clean sheets in the Champions League group stages with Atletico Madrid.

- BONATINI
- BEN YEDDER
- ASENSIO
- UMTITI
- BACCA
- MESSI
- LUIS
- SUAREZ
- OBLAK

- PAULINHO
- ILLARRAMENDI
- MARTINEZ
- ASPAS
- BUSQUETS
- ISCO
- GUEDES
- RONALDO
- GRIEZMANN

Sevilla forward **Wissam Ben Yedder** scored six goals in his first **17** La Liga games in **2017–18.**

ANSWERS ON PAGE 94.

ALL ABOUT BAYERN MUNICH

German clubs don't come any bigger than the brilliant Bayern Munich! The Bundesliga greats are a worldwide superpower with stacks of success.

PLAYER POWER

Sandro Wagner, James Rodriguez, Kingsley Coman and Mats Hummels all joined Bayern in the last couple of years. Added to experienced stars like Thomas Muller, Arjen Robben, Arturo Vidal and Franck Ribery, their squad's one of the best in Europe. Plus, Bayern have the goalscoring skills of Robert Lewandowski – one of the most dangerous strikers on the planet!

GERMAN GIANTS

Thanks to a record 28 German titles between 1932 and 2018, Bayern Munich's trophy cabinet is absolutely stuffed! The last time they finished outside of the top two was way back in 2007 and they now have six league championships in a row. With over 30 German cups and five Champions Leagues up to 2013, it's a huge shock if Bayern don't win at least one trophy every season.

STARS TO WATCH...

THOMAS MULLER
FORWARD
Goalscorer & creator

KINGSLEY COMAN
WINGER
Speedy & skilful

MANUEL NEUER
GOALKEEPER
Awesome saves & kicking

SANDRO WAGNER
STRIKER
Epic in the air

ROBERT LEWANDOWSKI

NICKNAME: The Bavarians
STADIUM: Allianz Arena
CAPACITY: 71,137
HOME KIT: Red
YEAR FOUNDED: 1900
CLUB LEGENDS: Franz Beckenbauer, Gerd Muller, Philipp Lahm, Sepp Maier, Lothar Matthaus

Robert Lewandowski first wore the Bayern No.9 in **2014** after moving from Bundesliga rivals Borussia Dortmund.

In 2015, Bayern's No.9 scored a record **five** Bundesliga goals in just **nine** minutes against Wolfsburg.

Lewandowski's a goal creator too, clocking up **94** assists in **397** appearances for club and country.

He helped Poland reach the **2018** World Cup by netting a European record of **16** goals in qualifying.

In **250** Bundesliga games, Robert smashed an unbelievable **171** goals!

Lewandowski moved into the top ten all-time Champions League goal scorers in 2018 with his **45th** strike in **67** games.

The Poland captain has been voted his country's Player of the Year **seven** times in a row!

In **2013** he blasted **four** goals in a Champions League semi-final for Borussia Dortmund against Real Madrid.

Robert needed just **136** games to crack in his **100th** Bayern Munich goal in all competitions.

CAPTAIN: Manuel Neuer **TOP SCORER:** Gerd Muller (533) **YOUNG STAR:** Christian Fruchtl

BORUSSIA DORTMUND

With Bundesliga and Champions League trophies, Borussia Dortmund can flex their muscles with the best clubs in Europe! Check out their top stats and stars.

GROUND FORCE

The atmosphere at the mighty Signal Iduna Park is unlike anywhere else in Germany! It's the biggest ground in the country, with its south stand alone housing 24,454 fans, and generates a monster sound when Dortmund turn on the style and hit the net. The stadium opened in 1974 and every Bundesliga player looks forward to running out at this legendary venue.

TROPHY TALK

Borussia Dortmund are a powerful European club, with impressive trophy counts at home and abroad. They've won three Bundesliga titles in the 21st century, with eight in total, plus nine major German cups up to 2017. In 1997, Dortmund were the first German club to win the Champions League and were runners-up to Bayern Munich in 2013.

STARS TO WATCH...

MARIO GOTZE
MIDFIELDER
Clever goalscorer

MARCO REUS
STRIKER
Ace attacking skills

MAXIMILIAN PHILIPP
STRIKER
Alert in the box

SOKRATIS PAPASTATHOPOULOS
DEFENDER
Out-muscles strikers

NICKNAME: The Black and Yellows
STADIUM: Signal Iduna Park
CAPACITY: 81,360
HOME KIT: Yellow and black
YEAR FOUNDED: 1909
CLUB LEGENDS: Matthias Sammer, Jurgen Klopp, Michael Zorc, Manfred Burgsmuller

EPIC ENGLAND STAR

Tricky teenager Jadon Sancho surprisingly left Manchester City in 2017 to make his mark in the Bundesliga. The midfielder helped England win the Under-17 World Cup and with Dortmund's No.7 shirt, Sancho's expected to become a key player for the German giants. He's full of slick skills and loves to burst forward to create and score goals!

CAPTAIN: Marcel Schmelzer **TOP SCORER:** Manfred Burgsmuller (135) **YOUNG STAR:** Sergio Gomez

ALL ABOUT RB LEIPZIG

An exciting team with an amazing success story in recent years – RB Leipzig are Bundesliga giants with a big future!

FAST FORWARD

RB Leipzig only formed in 2009 – you might have smelly footy socks nearly as old as that! They started out in the fifth division of German footy and by 2016 they'd stormed to the Bundesliga after four exciting promotions. The Bulls' first season in the top division was amazing – they won 20 games, collected 67 points and finished runners-up to Bayern Munich. It's never boring being a RB Leipzig fan!

CHAMPIONS LEAGUE

Just eight years after their very first game, RB Leipzig played in the Champions League! In the 2017-18 season the club won twice and drew one game in Group G, with striker Emil Forsberg scoring their first European goal. In the Europa League that season, The Bulls pulled off another shock by beating Serie A leaders Napoli. The Germans will definitely be a Euro force for years to come.

STARS TO WATCH...

DAYOT UPAMECANO
DEFENDER
Talented on the ball

TIMO WERNER
STRIKER
Star German goalscorer

YUSSUF POULSEN
STRIKER
Strong team player

PETER GULACSI
GOALKEEPER
Awesome shot-stopper

NICKNAME: The Bulls
STADIUM: Red Bull Arena
CAPACITY: 42,959
HOME KIT: Red and white
YEAR FOUNDED: 2009
CLUB LEGENDS: Ralph Hasenhuttl, Timo Werner, Naby Keita, Dominik Kaiser

NABY KEITA

Behind RB Leipzig's sensational Bundesliga rise was power-packed central midfielder, Naby Keita. The Guinea star joined the team in 2016 and hit 15 goals and ten assists in his first 57 games. He was like Lionel Messi and N'Golo Kante all rolled into one – a skilful attacking star who won the ball in the middle of the pitch for The Bulls. It's no surprise that Liverpool FC paid a huge transfer fee to bring him to Anfield in 2018!

RB LEIPZIG TIMELINE

2010 Oberliga champions
2011 Regionalliga fourth
2012 Regionalliga third
2013 Regionalliga champions
2014 3. Liga runners-up
2015 2. Bundesliga fifth
2016 2. Bundesliga runners-up
2017 Bundesliga runners-up

CAPTAIN: Willi Orban **SURPRISE SIGNING:** Ademola Lookman (loan) **YOUNG STAR:** Dayot Upamecano

ALL ABOUT SCHALKE

Let's jet over to the German city of Gelsenkirchen to check out the superstar players at Schalke!

TOP THILO

Schalke's defensive star is Thilo Kehrer. The German youngster has strength, vision, skill on the ball and has been a regular in the club's backline since 2016. Kehrer's not just an important centre-back, though. In 38 Bundesliga games for Schalke he played in eight positions! Even though he's comfortable in central midfield and even on the wing, Kehrer should keep his spot bossing Schalke's defence for many years to come.

TROPHY TALK

A big German club with a rich history, Schalke have seven top-flight titles. The last of these was back in 1958 and they finished as Bundesliga runners-up three times between 2005 and 2010. In 2011 they had a thrilling team and heroes like Raul, Edu, Manuel Neuer, Julian Draxler and Klass-Jan Huntelaar helped them reach the Champions League semi-finals.

STARS TO WATCH...

NABIL BENTALEB
MIDFIELDER
Ambitious attacker

GUIDO BURGSTALLER
STRIKER
Deadly in the box

NALDO
DEFENDER
Experienced & strong

AMINE HARIT
MIDFIELDER
Exciting goal creator

NICKNAME: The Royal Blues
STADIUM: Veltins Arena
CAPACITY: 62,271
HOME KIT: Blue and white
YEAR FOUNDED: 1904
CLUB LEGENDS: Klaus Fichtel, Klaus Fischer, Andreas Muller, Mesut Ozil, Hans Schmidt

YOUNG STARS

Schalke are famous for producing amazing young players. In Germany's 2014 World Cup winning squad, Mesut Ozil, Julian Draxler, Benedikt Howedes and Manuel Neuer had all starred for the club as kids! USA midfielder Weston McKennie is the latest youngster to break into the team and Leon Goretzka, who joined Bayern Munich in 2018, first played for Schalke aged just 18.

CAPTAIN: Ralf Fahrmann **TOP BUNDESLIGA SCORER:** Klaus Fischer (182) **YOUNG STAR:** Weston McKennie

NAME GAME

This club, whose name begins with **W**, were champions in **2009**.

Work out the names of these brilliant Bundesliga clubs by filling in the missing letters.

1

H _ _ T H _ B E _ _ I N

Based in Germany's capital city.

2

W O _ _ S B U _ _

A scary animal is the beginning of their name.

3

B _ _ _ R _ E V E _ _ _ S E N

Kevin Volland and Leon Bailey are ace goalscorers for this club.

4

E I _ T R A _ _ T F _ _ N K F _ _ T

High-flying German club, nicknamed The Eagles!

5

_ _ _ D E R B R _ _ _ _

This team plays at the Weser-Stadion.

ANSWERS ON PAGE 94.

WORLD SUPERSTARS FROM THE PAST

From Pele to Cruyff and Maradona to Maldini, discover why this bunch of brilliant world superstars are the biggest heroes from the past!

RONALDINHO

MAIN CLUBS: AC Milan, Barcelona, PSG
POSITION: Forward
COUNTRY: Brazil

- Super skilful winger or striker
- La Liga, Serie A and Champions League winner
- World Cup hero with Brazil in 2002

DIEGO MARADONA

MAIN CLUBS: Boca Juniors, Napoli, Barcelona
POSITION: STRIKER
COUNTRY: Argentina

- Lead Napoli to Serie A title in 1987 and 1990
- Superstar of the 1986 World Cup
- Strength, skills and epic dribbling

EUSEBIO

MAIN CLUB: Benfica
POSITION: Striker
COUNTRY: Portugal

- Incredible record of 727 goals in 715 Benfica games
- Golden Boot winner at 1966 World Cup
- Deadly hitman with 11 titles in Portugal

PELE

MAIN CLUB: Santos
POSITION: Striker
COUNTRY: Brazil

- Won World Cup in 1958, 1962 and 1970
- Deadly accurate in front of goal
- Career record of 1,281 goals

ALFREDO DI STEFANO

MAIN CLUB: Real Madrid
POSITION: Striker
COUNTRY: Spain and Argentina

- Five European Cup victories
- Superstar striker in 1950s and '60s
- Powerful, with laser-like shooting

GEORGE BEST

MAIN CLUB: Manchester United
POSITION: Forward
COUNTRY: Northern Ireland

- Red Devils megastar in 1960s and '70s
- Deadly dribbling, speed, tricks and shooting
- 179 goals in 470 Manchester United games

I've got more medals than you've had hot dinners!

PAOLO MALDINI

CLUB: AC Milan
POSITION: Defender
COUNTRY: Italy

- Played 902 games and won 26 trophies with Milan
- Cool on the ball, tough, with a sweet left foot
- Five times Champions League winner

PAST HEROES

GERD MULLER

MAIN CLUB: Bayern Munich
POSITION: Striker
COUNTRY: Germany

- Club record 533 goals for Bayern
- Five Bundesliga and three European Cup titles
- World Cup winner in 1974

MICHEL PLATINI

MAIN CLUBS: Juventus, St-Etienne
POSITION: Forward
COUNTRY: France

- Serie A and European Cup winner
- Amazing goalscorer and leader
- Speed, skills and intelligence

FRANZ BECKENBAUER

MAIN CLUB: Bayern Munich
POSITION: Defender
COUNTRY: Germany

- Stylish centre-back and sweeper
- Three European Cups and five Bundesligas
- World Cup winner as player and coach

RONALDO

MAIN CLUBS: Real Madrid, Inter Milan
POSITION: Striker
COUNTRY: Brazil

- World Cup star in 1998, 2002, 2006
- Amazing speed, tricks and shooting
- Two La Liga titles with Real Madrid

Zidane starred for France at the 2006, 2002 and 1998 World Cup.

MIROSLAV KLOSE

MAIN CLUBS: Lazio, Bayern Munich, Werder Bremen
POSITION: Striker
COUNTRY: Germany

- Germany legend with 16 World Cup finals goals
- Record 71 strikes in 137 international games
- Awesome header of the ball

ROBERTO BAGGIO

MAIN CLUBS: AC Milan, Juventus, Fiorentina
POSITION: Forward
COUNTRY: Italy

- Serie A winner with Juventus and Milan
- Amazing dribbling and free-kicks
- Starred at 1998, 1994 and 1990 World Cup

JOHAN CRUYFF

MAIN CLUBS: Ajax, Barcelona
POSITION: Forward
COUNTRY: Netherlands

- Stylish, skilful and great vision
- Three European Player of the Year awards
- European Cup winner as player and coach

ZINEDINE ZIDANE

MAIN CLUBS: Real Madrid, Juventus
POSITION: Midfielder
COUNTRY: France

- Three World Player of the Year trophies
- World Cup and Champions League winner
- Magical skills, control, power and passing

FACE THE FACTS!

1

CLUE: I'm a striker and my initials are KM.

ANSWER:..

2

CLUE: I used to star for Liverpool FC!

ANSWER:..

3

CLUE: I love robbin' defenders.

ANSWER:..

4

CLUE: I swapped Spurs' white for Real Madrid's white!

ANSWER:..

Work out who these cool Champions League legends are from the funny photos and clues!

5

CLUE: I 'keep' starring in Italy!

ANSWER:..

6

CLUE: I'm a midfielder and my initials are 'CP'.

ANSWER:..

7

CLUE: I cost £200 million!

ANSWER:..

8

CLUE: I'm a 'real' good captain.

ANSWER:..

ANSWERS ON PAGE 94.

ALL ABOUT JUVENTUS

Juventus boss Serie A! The Italian masters have fantastic players, bags of trophies and amazing fans. Take a close look at the awesome Italians...

PLAYER POWER

Juventus' squad is boosted by many of Serie A's top stars. After selling Paul Pogba to Manchester United in 2016, they bought striker Gonzalo Higuain for a huge £75 million. Higuan scored 24 league goals in his first season and he's supported in attack by Paulo Dybala and Mario Mandzukic. Gianluigi Buffon has been a legendary keeper since joining in 2001 and Andrea Barzagli and Giorgio Chiellini proved a tough centre-back duo.

TROPHY TALK

In 2017, Juventus picked up a record 33rd Italian top-flight championship. It was also the first time any club had won six Serie A titles in a row! The Old Lady are European heavyweights with two Champions League crowns, but they have lost Europe's biggest final seven times, including 2017 and 2015. Up to 2017, Juve also had 12 Coppa Italia and seven Italian Super Cup trophies. There's plenty of silverware on show!

STARS TO WATCH...

MIRALEM PJANIC
MIDFIELDER
Cool head bosses games

JUAN CUADRADO
WINGER
Speed & slick right foot

SAMI KHEDIRA
MIDFIELDER
Brings goals & epic passing

GONZALO HIGUAIN
STRIKER
Pure goal machine

PAULO DYBALA

NICKNAME: The Old Lady
STADIUM: Allianz Stadium
CAPACITY: 41,500
HOME KIT: Black and white
YEAR FOUNDED: 1897
CLUB LEGENDS: Zinedine Zidane, Michel Platini, Gianluigi Buffon, Alessandro Del Piero, Roberto Baggio, Dino Zoff

Forward **Paulo Dybala** first wore No.10 for Juventus in August 2017. He had No.21 when he joined from Palermo in 2015.

Before Juventus, the attacker spent three seasons in Serie A with **Palermo**.

He scored **45** Serie A goals in his first **86** games for Juve.

Dybala also plays for Argentina and made his first international appearance in **2015**.

The Juventus No.10 is a speedy forward and can reach speeds of **29 km** per hour on the pitch!

He was born in November **1993**.

His first Champions League goal was against Bayern Munich in **2016**.

He's a **free-kick** king who loves to whip the ball over the wall!

In **2017–18**, Dybala scored **12** of his first **15** Serie A goals with his **left** foot.

His favourite foot is his **left**.

CAPTAIN: Giorgio Chiellini **BIG BUY:** Gonzalo Higuain (£75M in 2016) **YOUNG STAR:** Rodrigo Bentancur

ALL ABOUT AC MILAN

In the red and black half of Milan, this mighty club have a huge history of winning Serie A and European titles in style!

EURO STARS

AC Milan are tied with rivals Inter Milan on 18 Italian title wins. Their last championship was in 2011 and their first back in 1901. Il Rossoneri are the most successful Italian club in European competition though, lifting the Champions League seven times between 1963 and 2007. They were one of the world's top teams in the late 1980s and 1990s, taking European silverware in 1989, 1990 and 1994, plus six Serie A crowns from 1988 to 1999.

PLAYER POWER

Cutrone just turned 20 in January 2018, but he's developing into a big star for AC Milan. He has power, skill and loves playing for his boyhood club! Bonucci and Alessio Romagnoli are like a brick wall in defence, with right-back Davide Calabria bombing forward at every opportunity. Midfielders Franck Kessie, Lucas Biglia and Jack Bonaventura have strength and tackling with clever attacking passes.

STARS TO WATCH...

SUSO
MIDFIELDER
Cool creative talent

GIANLUIGI DONNARUMMA
GOALKEEPER
Italy's top young stopper

HAKAN CALHANOGLU
MIDFIELDER
Playmaker & set-piece star

FRANCK KESSIE
MIDFIELDER
Power-packed & super stamina

NICKNAME: Il Rossoneri
STADIUM: San Siro
CAPACITY: 80,018
HOME KIT: Red and black
YEAR FOUNDED: 1899
CLUB LEGENDS: Paolo Maldini, Arrigo Sacchi, Fabio Capello, Marco Van Basten, Gunnar Nordahl

GAME PLAN

After AC Milan had new owners in 2017 and bought experienced defender Leonardo Bonucci from Juventus for £35 million, they had mixed results. Manager Gennaro Gattuso arrived in November and took the team on a long unbeaten run from the start of 2018. Gattuso's defensive 4-3-3 formation made them much stronger at the back, with young striker Patrick Cutrone looking sharp up front.

Milan are muscling in on the action!

Cutrone played his first game for AC Milan in 2017 aged 19.

CAPTAIN: Leonardo Bonucci **TOP SCORER:** Gunnar Nordahl (221) **YOUNG STAR:** Patrick Cutrone

ALL ABOUT INTER MILAN

Inter Milan haven't won Serie A since 2010, but they're still a talented and dangerous team...especially with Mauro Icardi banging in the goals!

TROPHY TALK

Before Juventus dominated Serie A, Inter Milan were the team at the top. Il Nerazzurri scooped five titles in a row between 2006 and 2010 and now have 18 in the bag. Their biggest trophy in recent years was the Champions League in 2010, when they beat Bayern Munich 2-0 in the final. That year Inter won an historic treble of Serie A, Coppa Italia and Champions League.

MILAN RIVALRY

The Milan derby between Inter and AC is one of the most exciting clashes on the planet! In the first Serie A meeting in 2017-18, Inter grabbed all three points thanks to Mauro Icardi's penalty in the 90th minute. The teams also battled in the Champions League in 2005 and 2003, with AC Milan on top each time. The clubs both play at the San Siro stadium, so derby games are very special for both sets of fans!

STARS TO WATCH...

IVAN PERISIC
WINGER
Epic attacking skills

MILAN SKRINIAR
DEFENDER
Inter's top centre-back

BORJA VALERO
MIDFIELDER
Box-to-box style

ANTONIO CANDREVA
MIDFIELDER
Clever skills in midfield

NICKNAME: Il Nerazzurri
STADIUM: San Siro
CAPACITY: 80,018
HOME KIT: Blue and black
YEAR FOUNDED: 1908
CLUB LEGENDS: Javier Zanetti, Jose Mourinho, Ronaldo, Giuseppe Meazza, Walter Zenga

INCREDIBLE ICARDI

Argentina striker Mauro Icardi joined Inter Milan in 2013 from Sampdoria – and he hasn't stopped scoring goals since! Icardi struck 78 from 146 in his first four seasons and racked up 18 in his first 22 Serie A games in 2017–18. He was made club captain in 2015 and with such deadly shooting skills, it's no surprise Manchester United and Real Madrid have been linked with a big transfer move for him.

Look mum, I didn't get my shirt dirty today!

CAPTAIN: Mauro Icardi **TOP SCORER:** Giuseppe Meazza (284) **YOUNG STAR:** Yann Karamoh

ALL ABOUT NAPOLI

Napoli are back in the Serie A big time! Discover the stars, style and success of the famous club in southern Italy.

SERIE A STYLE KINGS

Napoli are probably the most entertaining Serie A team. Their style, cheekily nicknamed 'Sarrismo' after the coach, is a bit like Spain's tika-taka passing game. Napoli can play the ball coolly from defence, or launch speedy counter attacks through clever midfielders like Marek Hamsik, Allan and Piotr Zielinski. Their goal-getters Dries Mertens, Jose Callejon and Lorenzo Insigne then do plenty of damage in the box!

TROPHY TALK

Napoli only secured their first Serie A title in 1987, with a second coming just three years later. They've been in the shadow of clubs like Juventus, Roma and the Milan duo for a long time. But, the Gli Azzurri made an awesome championship charge in 2018 under manager Maurizio Sarri and caught the eye with their slick attacking play. Napoli were Serie A runners-up in 2016 and finished third in 2017.

STARS TO WATCH...

KALIDOU KOULIBALY
DEFENDER
Towering centre-back

JORGINHO
MIDFIELDER
All-action passing & moving

DRIES MERTENS
STRIKER
Lethal in the box

PEPE REINA
GOALKEEPER
Huge experience

NICKNAME: Gli Azzurri
STADIUM: Stadio San Paolo
CAPACITY: 60,240
HOME KIT: Blue and white
YEAR FOUNDED: 1904
CLUB LEGENDS: Diego Maradona, Giuseppe Bruscolotti, Marek Hamsik

SUPER STRIKERS

Sarri has turned winger Mertens into the club's latest goal-crazy striker! The Belgian grabbed 28 Serie A strikes in 2016–17, with 17 from his first 27 appearances the following season. Mertens is one of a long line of epic goalscorers at Napoli recently. Edinson Cavani and Gonzalo Higuain blasted nearly 150 league goals between them before moving to PSG and Juventus.

These new anti-gravity boots are epic!

CAPTAIN: Marek Hamsik **TOP SCORER:** Maeik Hamsik (119+) **YOUNG STAR**: Amadou Diawara

SERIE A

HIT OR MISS?

Boo hoo! I missed! Sob, sob!

Look closely at these footy photos from Italy and guess whether a goal was scored or not!

1

Atalanta's Alejandro Gomez curls a shot from the edge of the box.

- IT WAS A GOAL.
- IT WASN'T A GOAL.

2

Sampdoria forward Fabio Quagliarella blasts at Fiorentina's goal.

- IT WAS A GOAL.
- IT WASN'T A GOAL.

3

Ciro Immobile takes a penalty for Lazio against Roma.

IT WAS A GOAL.

IT WASN'T A GOAL.

4

AC Milan's Alessio Romagnoli battles the Sassuolo keeper.

IT WAS A GOAL.

IT WASN'T A GOAL.

5

Paulo Dybala bends a free-kick for Juventus against Lazio in Turin.

IT WAS A GOAL.

IT WASN'T A GOAL.

ANSWERS ON PAGE 94.

ALL ABOUT

PARIS SAINT-GERMAIN

Paris Saint-Germain have plenty of heroes and pick up trophies every season. Find out why the French giants are totally fantastique!

TROPHY TALK

After four Ligue 1 titles in a row between 2013 and 2016, Paris Saint-Germain were beaten to the top spot by Monaco in 2017. But they charged back to their seventh championship in 2018, with Edinson Cavani, Kylian Mbappe and Neymar cracking in goals left, right and centre! PSG also won 11 French Cups and seven League Cups up to 2017 and reached the Champions League quarter-finals from 2013 to 2016.

PLAYER POWER

You'll see more stars in PSG's mega-expensive squad than if you look through a telescope at night! As well as their awesome attacking trio, Thiago Silva, Dani Alves, Angel Di Maria, Julian Draxler and Adrien Rabiot bossed Ligue 1 in 2018 as manager Unai Emery cruised to more trophies. PSG's talented team created an amazing 347 goal attempts in their first 35 league and Champions League games last season!

STARS TO WATCH...

EDINSON CAVANI
STRIKER
Penalty-box predator

THIAGO SILVA
DEFENDER
Cool head & top tackling

MARCO VERRATTI
MIDFIELDER
Ace playmaker

JULIAN DRAXLER
MIDFIELDER
Skilful, with awesome energy

NICKNAME: PSG
STADIUM: Parc des Princes
CAPACITY: 47,929
HOME KIT: Blue
YEAR FOUNDED: 1970
CLUB LEGENDS: Zlatan Ibrahimovic, Ronaldinho, George Weah, Edinson Cavani

His full name is **Neymar da Silva Santos Junior**.

Paris Saint-Germain's No.10 joined from Barcelona for a world-record **£200** million in **2017**!

In his first **20** Ligue 1 games, Neymar struck **19** goals.

The Brazilian cracked in **seven** goals in just six Champions League games for PSG.

He hit the net on his debut for Brazil in **2010**, aged just **18**.

In January **2018**, Neymar scored **four** goals in an **8–0** Ligue 1 thrashing of Dijon.

In **2011** he won the FIFA Puskas Award for a stunning solo goal for Santos against Flamengo.

At Barcelona he won **eight** major trophies, including La Liga twice and the Champions League in **2015**.

In **83** Brazil appearances he has already smashed in **53** goals.

CAPTAIN: Thiago Silva **TOP SCORER:** Edinson Cavani (160+) **YOUNG STARS:** Tim Weah, Kylian Mbappe (on loan)

ALL ABOUT MONACO

In the sunny south of France, Monaco are full of glitz, glamour, goals and trophies! Take your sunglasses off and check them out!

FRENCH FANCIES

Monaco's rise to become Ligue 1 champions and Champions League semi-finalists in 2017 was one of the biggest footy stories of the year. Sadly, heroes Kylian Mbappe, Benjamin Mendy and Tiemoue Bakayoko left Monaco soon after and the club couldn't repeat their European success the following season. But they fought Marseille and Lyon all the way for the runner-up spot, with stars like Radamel Falcao and Keita Balde impressing the fans.

PLAYER POWER

Europe's big clubs are once again eyeing up the talent at Monaco! Powerful young forward Keita Balde collected eight goals and six assists in 29 games and exciting 16-year-old striker Pietro Pellegri arrived from Genoa in January 2018. Youri Tielemans is a skilful Belgian midfielder and winger Thomas Lemar nearly joined Arsenal as a replacement for Alexis Sanchez.

STARS TO WATCH...

FABINHO
DEFENDER
Hard working and scores goals

JOAO MOUTINHO
MIDFIELDER
Clever footwork and skills

RONY LOPES
FORWARD
Speedy Portuguese attacker

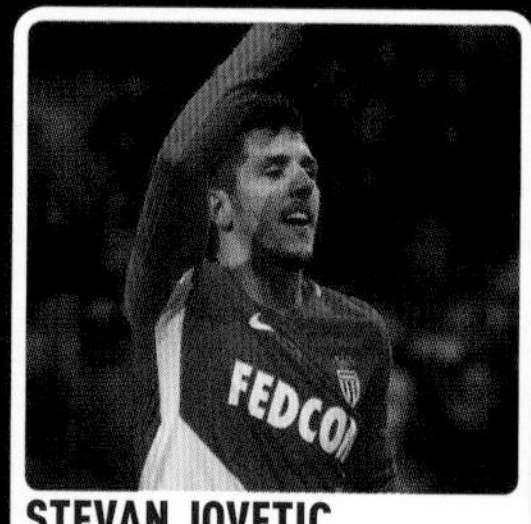

STEVAN JOVETIC
STRIKER
Always troubles defenders

NICKNAME: Les Rouges et Blancs
STADIUM: Stade Louis II
CAPACITY: 18,523
HOME KIT: Red and white
YEAR FOUNDED: 1924
CLUB LEGENDS: Delio Onnis, Thierry Henry, George Weah, Patrice Evra, Emmanuel Petit

MR MONACO

Even though he turned 32 in 2018, Colombian striker Radamel Falcao remains the key man for Monaco! The captain joined the club in 2013, having crashed in 142 goals for Atletico Madrid and Porto, and struck 11 goals in his first 19 matches in France. By March 2018 his record stood at 66 in just 92 appearances to prove he's still up there with the best strikers in the game.

Falcao also played **36** games for Chelsea and Manchester United.

CAPTAIN: Radamel Falcao **TOP SCORER:** Delio Onnis (223) **YOUNG STAR:** Pietro Pellegri

ALL ABOUT MARSEILLE

In their famous white kit and based at their impressive Stade Velodrome, Marseille are a powerful force in French and European footy!

PLAYER POWER

Premier League fans are used to seeing former West Ham winger Dimitri Payet whipping free-kicks into the box and setting up goals. He's now doing just that at Marseille, with ten assists and five goals in his first 32 games in 2017-18. Forward Valere Germain and midfielder Morgan Sanson have chipped in with lots of goals too – and they also have the special powers of Florian Thauvin!

TROPHY TALK

In 1993, French club Marseille won the Champions League and were also runners-up in 1991. They scooped four Ligue 1 titles in a row between 1989 and 1992 and were one of the most powerful outfits in Europe back then. In total, Les Olympiens have nine championships, winning the last one in 2010, so they are a club used to winning big games and big trophies!

STARS TO WATCH...

MORGAN SANSON
MIDFIELDER
Creative attacker

STEVE MANDANDA
GOALKEEPER
Great reflexes & power

LUIZ GUSTAVO
MIDFIELDER
Tackling & shooting skills

CLINTON N'JIE
MIDFIELDER
Sharp & energetic

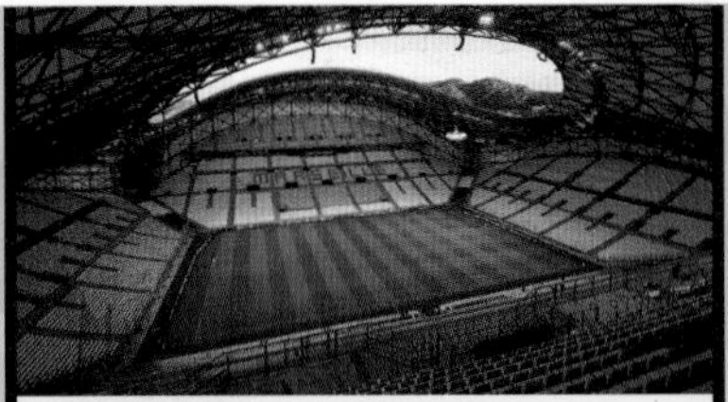

NICKNAME: Les Olympiens
STADIUM: Stade Velodrome
CAPACITY: 67,394
HOME KIT: White
YEAR FOUNDED: 1899
CLUB LEGENDS: Jean-Pierre Papin, Gunnar Andersson, Josip Skoblar, Mario Zatelli, Chris Waddle

TOP THAUVIN

Winger or forward Thauvin scored zero Premier League goals for Newcastle in 2015-16. But, back at Marseille the Frenchman has become a goalscoring megastar! Cutting in from the right, his epic skills allow Thauvin to drive at defenders and curl left-foot shots or to slip a clever pass forward. He's become one of the most prized players in Ligue 1. Newcastle fans must be crying their eyes out!

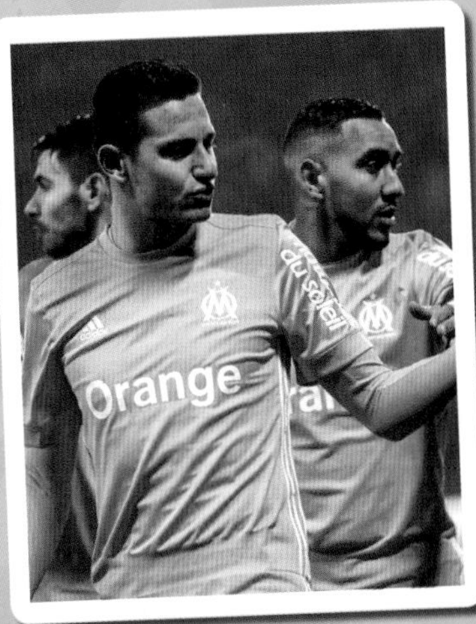

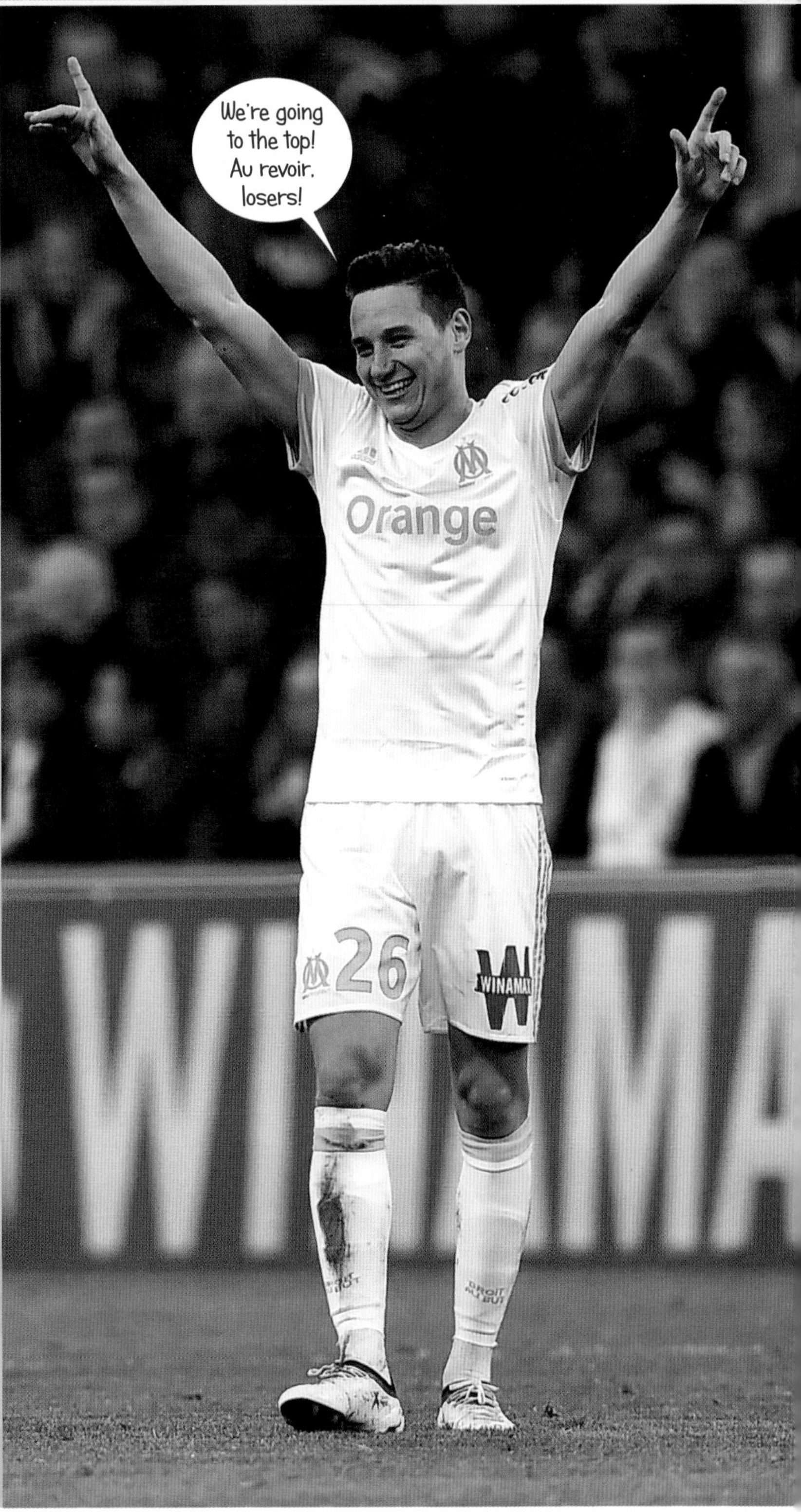
We're going to the top! Au revoir, losers!
Orange
26
WINAMAX

Orange

CAPTAIN: Dimitri Payet **TOP SCORER:** Gunnar Andersson (194) **YOUNG STAR:** Boubacar Kamara

ALL ABOUT LYON

With some of the most fearsome forwards in France, Lyon could be heading back to taking Ligue 1 and Europe by storm!

GAME PLAN

Even though they sold star striker Alexandre Lacazette to Arsenal in 2017, Lyon have remained a lethal attacking unit. Mariano Diaz usually leads a three-man strikeforce for Les Gones, with three midfielders behind giving the perfect balance of passing, tackling and power. Manager Bruno Genesio pushes his full-backs, Kenny Tete and Ferland Mendy, forward whenever he can to create more width and get crosses into the box.

TROPHY TALK

Even the all-conquering PSG can't match one of Lyon's incredible Ligue 1 records! Lyon won seven titles in a row between 2002 and 2008, and they dominated French footy at the start of the century. They reached the Champions League semi-finals in 2010 and the quarter-finals in 2004, 2005 and 2006. At their shiny new Groupama Stadium, Lyon are a match for any French or European team.

STARS TO WATCH...

TANGUY NDOMBELE
MIDFIELDER
Powerful & creative

BERTRAND TRAORE
FORWARD
Livewire skills & speed

HOUSSEM AOUAR
MIDFIELDER
Versatile, with epic energy

FERLAND MENDY
DEFENDER
Tough & top at tackling

NICKNAME: Les Gones
STADIUM: Groupama Stadium
CAPACITY: 59,186
HOME KIT: White, red and blue
YEAR FOUNDED: 1950
CLUB LEGENDS: Juninho Pernambucano, Serge Chiesa, Gregory Coupet, Sonny Anderson

PLAYER POWER

After 28 league games in 2017-18, Lyon's dazzling duo of Diaz and Nabil Fekir had scored 16 goals each! Former Manchester United forward Memphis Depay also joins the attack, hitting nine goals in 28 games. Captain Fekir was one of France's hottest players in 2018. He's a demon dribbler and a master free-kick taker, scoring against PSG, Marseille and Monaco from set pieces last season. His strike from the halfway line against Bordeaux was incredible!

Sorry, I didn't see you asleep down there!

CAPTAIN: Nabil Fekir **TOP LIGUE 1 SCORER:** Fleury Di Nallo (182) **YOUNG STAR:** Houssem Aouar

Tackle these teasers about the biggest stars and clubs in France!

LIGUE 1 LADS!

PREMIER PICKS

Fill in the names of these ex-Premier League players.

1

RAFAEL DA..................................

2

ANGEL ....

3

DIAFRA ....

CLOSE CALL

Can you tell who this former Ligue 1 star is, just from this close-up pic and clue?

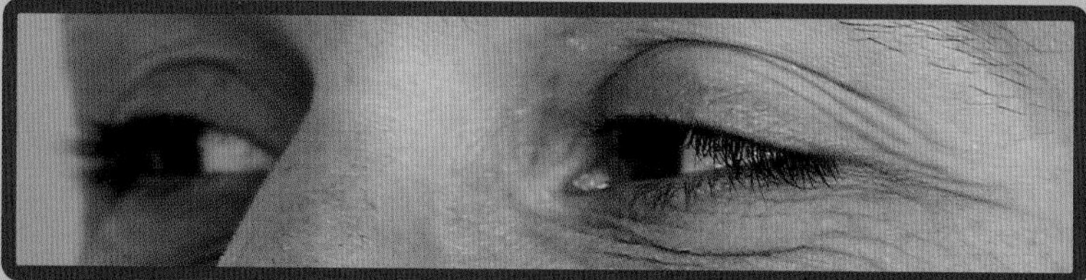

CLUE...

I scored 156 goals playing in the French capital.

ANSWER:...............................

PAYING THE PENALTY

Monaco striker Radamel Falcao takes a penalty against Lyon, but which is the real ball?

THE REAL BALL IS:

GUESS THE YEAR

In which year did these things happen? Take your pick from the list → **2016 2008 2013**

David Beckham signs for PSG.

ANSWER:...

Lyon win their seventh Ligue 1 trophy.

ANSWER:...

Mario Balotelli plays his first game for Nice.

ANSWER:...

ANSWERS ON PAGE 94.

PLAY TO WIN!

As every football manager knows, you need strategy as well as top players to be a winner. Here are five top tips to help you collect and play like a pro. You'll soon be a Match Attax master!

1 101 – THE ULTIMATE MATCH ATTAX CARD

Look out for the new 101-rated card in packets. The 101-er is unbeatable so it's a no-brainer to get one into your line-up!

2 AWAY KITS AND HAT-TRICK HEROES!

Away Kit cards feature players in their team's alternative strip and are a must-have for your team. These cool cards could score you two goals meaning playing from home need never be a problem again. Also don't miss out on Hat-Trick Heroes, exclusively available in Match Attax Extra, featuring players who've scored trebles throughout the season. They could score you three goals!

3 SUPER SUBS!

Each team has 11 players and 3 subs so if you want to switch things up, you'll need a good impact player coming off the bench. You can surprise an opponent and turn the game into your favour with a well-timed sub!

4 TALKING TACTICS

Change the game with Tactic cards. These super collectable game-changers include injury, referee and agent cards. They can damage an opponent's score, increase your transfer budget, make an opponent swap their player and even boost your cards. You're allowed to use two of them in each match so get them into your squad to take the win!

Let's go, it's time to up the game!

5 ATTACKING DEFENDERS, DEFENSIVE ATTACKERS!

Look out for players who are good in attack and defence, mainly all-rounder midfielders and flying full-backs like Paul Pogba and Marcos Alonso! These guys can spring a shock on an opponent out of nowhere!

NEW MATCH ATTAX APP!

You can now get the new Match Attax app to collect, swap and play with thousands of other fans! All you need to do is:

STEP 1. Search PL Match Attax on your App store.

STEP 2. Download the new Match Attax App.

STEP 3. Scan codes found in Match Attax packets to get free digital cards.

STEP 4. Build your digital team and join the fun!

SWAP & PLAY TOUR

If you want to find out more about Match Attax, come along to one of our Swap & Play Tour events! You'll be able to swap cards to complete your collection, play games against other collectors and even take part in the Match Attax World Championships!

For more information about dates and events go to **toppsfootball.com**

Get ready for spectacular strikes by some of the biggest world stars of all time!

BEST GOALS EVER!

MIKAEL NILSSON

IFK GOTEBORG v PSV Eindhoven
March 17, 1993

- Incredible bending free-kick by the defender
- Nilsson smacked the ball with his right foot
- It sliced through the air and curled past the keeper

ZLATAN IBRAHIMOVIC

PARIS SAINT-GERMAIN v Bastia
October 19, 2013

- Captain Ibrahimovic showed great technique
- Crazy flicked backheel volley
- PSG cruise to 4-0 victory

MARTA

SANTOS v Juventus
January 30, 2011

- Brazil's greatest women's player
- Dribbled past three and then the keeper
- Cheeky flick into an open goal

MARIO MANDZUKIC
JUVENTUS v Real Madrid, 2017
Epic overhead volley.

GEORGE WEAH
AC MILAN v Verona 1996
Rapid run from his own box.

ZINEDINE ZIDANE

Bayer Leverkusen v REAL MADRID
May 15, 2002

- Frenchman fired an epic long-range volley
- He helped Real win the Champions League final
- Incredible technique to strike the ball

Get me a tissue - I've dribbled everywhere!

JOHAN CRUYFF

AJAX v Helmond Sport
December 5, 1982

- Cruyff tapped his penalty to the side
- Team-mate Olsen rushed into box
- Cruyff took cheeky return to score

LIONEL MESSI

BARCELONA v Real Sociedad
December 12, 2010

- Fantastic dribble and finish in 5-0 win
- Skipped by four players in the box
- Arrowed clever shot back across the goal

DENNIS BERGKAMP

HOLLAND v Argentina, 1998
Control and cool finish in the box.

ESTEBAN CAMBIASSO

ARGENTINA v Serbia & Montenegro, 2006
Amazing team move and goal.

GOAL HEROES

LIONEL MESSI

BARCELONA v Getafe
April 18, 2007

- The teenager took the ball in his own half
- Steered and slid past five players
- Drove the ball into the net

RONALDO

Compostela v BARCELONA
October 18, 1997

- Power, skill and accuracy on show
- Ronaldo won the ball in the other half
- Raced to goal, beat four tackles and finished

CRISTIANO RONALDO

Rayo Vallecano v REAL MADRID
February 26, 2012

- Quick thinking by the Real legend
- Amazing backheel a long way from the goal
- Ronaldo fired Real to the 2012 title

MARCO VAN BASTEN

HOLLAND v Soviet Union, 1988
Sweet volley from a tight angle.

JAY-JAY OKOCHA

EINTRACHT FRANKFURT v Karlsruher, 1993
Twisting and turning in the area.

RIVALDO

BARCELONA v Valencia

June 17, 2001

- Spectacular overhead kick in 89th minute
- Brazilian scores winner and hat-trick goal
- Secured Barca's spot in the Champions League

DIEGO MARADONA

England v ARGENTINA

June 22, 1986

- Stunning solo strike in World Cup quarter-final
- The Napoli star dribbled from his own half
- Beat four challenges and shot past Peter Shilton

Grafite's goal helped Wolfsburg extend their unbeaten run to **nine** games.

GRAFITE

WOLFSBURG v Bayern Munich

April 4, 2009

- Super Skilful strike in 5-1 win
- Grafite dazzled and dribbled into the area
- Brilliant backheel past the keeper

ROBERTO CARLOS
BRAZIL v France, 1997
Swerving free-kick.

CARLOS ALBERTO
BRAZIL v Italy, 1970
Team move and crisp finish.

ALL ABOUT PRIMEIRA LIGA

SPORTING LISBON

Let's fly into Portugal to check out the biggest clubs and some of their best players, starting with the superstars at Sporting Lisbon...

GAME PLAN

Manager Jorge Jesus actually joined Sporting from their great Lisbon rivals Benfica, where he won a record ten trophies in just six seasons. In 2017-18, Jesus' Sporting relied heavily on the goals of Holland striker Bas Dost. He scored an impressive 20 league strikes in his first 21 games and no other forward at the club came close to matching that. In 2018, Sporting's usual 4-4-2 setup was bossed by star midfielder William Carvalho.

TROPHY TALK

Along with Porto and Benfica, Sporting Lisbon are one of the big three leading clubs in Portugal's Primeira Liga. They have notched up 18 championship victories between 1941 and 2002 and 18 Portuguese Cup wins up to 2015. Sporting lifted the European Cup Winners' Cup in 1964 and were runners-up in the UEFA Cup in 2005, when they lost at their own ground to CSKA Moscow.

STARS TO WATCH...

GELSON MARTINS
MIDFIELDER
Eye-catching winger

BAS DOST
STRIKER
Powerful & deadly

RUI PATRICIO
GOALKEEPER
Sporting's acrobatic No.1

MARCOS ACUNA
MIDFIELDER
Skilful Argentine international

NICKNAME: Lions
STADIUM: Estadio Jose Alvalade
CAPACITY: 50,095
HOME KIT: Green and white
YEAR FOUNDED: 1906
CLUB LEGENDS: Fernando Peyroteo, Liedson, Hilario, Mario Jardel, Cristiano Ronaldo

My second favourite sport is team wrestling!

PLAYER POWER

Carvalho has become one of the best all-action midfielders in Portugal since making his debut in 2011. He's a defensive powerhouse who doesn't hit the net very often, but he's ace at winning the ball and releasing his team's attackers. Bas Dost is Sporting's goal king. The giant striker only just missed out on the European Golden Shoe in 2017 when Lionel Messi pipped him to the prize. Gelson Martins and Bruno Fernandes are the main creative force.

CAPTAIN: William Carvalho **TOP SCORER:** Fernando Peyroteo (544) **YOUNG STAR:** Rafael Leao

ALL ABOUT BENFICA

Benfica have been the team to beat in Portugal recently! Take a quick look at their awesome records, stats, stars and success.

DECADE DOMINATION

The 2010s have been pretty good for the Portugal footy giants! Having won only two titles in the 1990s and one in the first decade this century, Benfica's 2017 success was their fourth in a row – a new record for the club. Their Champions League campaign in 2017-18 was a nightmare though as they lost all six group games. Manager Rui Vitoria joined in 2015 and in 2018, preferred to use a 4-3-3 system, with Jonas supported in attack by Franco Cervi and Eduardo Salvio.

TROPHY TALK

In 2017, Benfica stormed to a record 36th Primeira Liga title as well as doing the Double by securing the Portuguese Cup. The Lisbon club's first top-flight crown came in 1936 and they have over 60 league and cup championships in their huge trophy cabinet. Benfica's greatest trophies are their two European Cups from 1961 and 1962. They beat Spanish rivals Barcelona and Real Madrid as they became one of the world's greatest teams!

STARS TO WATCH...

PIZZI
MIDFIELDER
Links well with Jonas

EDUARDO SALVIO
WINGER
Dribbles & attacks

ANDRE ALMEIDA
DEFENDER
Solid & strong

FRANCO CERVI
MIDFIELDER
Clever touches & vision

JONAS

NICKNAME: Eagles
STADIUM: Estadio da Luz
CAPACITY: 64,642
HOME KIT: Red and white
YEAR FOUNDED: 1904
CLUB LEGENDS: Eusebio, Nene,

CAPTAIN: Luisao **TOP SCORER:** Eusebio (473) **YOUNG STAR:** Mile Svilar

ALL ABOUT PORTO

Portugal's Porto have a record to match most major European clubs! Discover everything you need to know about the Dragons.

CAPITAL CLASHES

Either Porto or the Lisbon duo of Sporting or Benfica have won every Primeira Liga since 2001- the year that Boavista won a shock championship. Porto only lost once against Benfica in seven league games between May 2014 and December 2017. In 2010 they bashed Benfica 5-0, with deadly double act Falcao and Hulk scoring twice each. They were undefeated against Sporting in 2017-18 and hit five past them in the Portuguese Cup in 2010.

EUROPEAN ROYALTY

Porto can proudly call themselves Portugal's princes of Europe! In total they've won five major European trophies, including the Champions League in 2004 and 1987. They bagged the Europa League in 2011 and 2003, plus the European Super Cup in 1987 and two Intercontinental Cups. Throw in their 27 league titles up to 2013 and they have quite a trophy collection!

STARS TO WATCH...

HECTOR HERRERA
MIDFIELDER
Cool-headed captain

YACINE BRAHIMI
MIDFIELDER
Epic left foot

OTAVIO
MIDFIELDER
Exciting skills & potential

JESUS CORONA
WINGER
Top crowd-pleaser

NICKNAME: Dragons
STADIUM: Estadio do Dragao
CAPACITY: 50,033
HOME KIT: Blue and white
YEAR FOUNDED: 1893
CLUB LEGENDS: Vitor Baia, Joao Pinto, Jose Mourinho, Mario Jardel

Time to score an im-porto-ant goal. Ha, ha!

PLAYER POWER

Vincent Aboubakar and Moussa Marega have been two of the top goal scorers in Portugal in 2018! The double act had struck over 35 times in the league by early March, with Aboubakar also hitting five in the Champions League. Tiquinho and Yacine Brahimi are also reliable scorers and creators for Porto. Felipe, Alex Telles, Ricardo Pereira and Marcano keep things solid at the back so Hector Herrera and Jesus Corona can wreck havoc going forward from the midfield.

CAPTAIN: Hector Herrera **TOP LEAGUE SCORER:** Fernando Gomes (355) **YOUNG STAR:** Diogo Dalot

HEAD TO TOE

Can you match the top half of these Primeira Liga players with the correct bottom half? It's a full on mega match-up madness!

1 Moussa Marega, Porto
2 William Carvalho, Sporting Lisbon
3 Paulinho, Sporting Braga
4 Franco Cervi, Benfica
5 Raphinha, Vitoria Guimaraes
6 Fabricio, Portimonense
7 Helder Guedes, Rio Ave
8 Bas Dost, Sporting Lisbon
9 Jonas, Benfica
10 Vincent Aboubakar, Porto
11 Jardel, Benfica
12 Ricardo Horta, Sporting Braga

ANSWERS ON PAGE 94.

ALL ABOUT AJAX

The Eredivisie is Holland's top league and is packed with exciting players and talented teams. The biggest and best is Ajax, from the capital Amsterdam.

TROPHY TALK

This could take a while! Dutch super club Ajax are a world-famous outfit, winning the European Cup three times in a row between 1971 and 1973, and the Champions League in 1995. The Amsterdam team also has won the European Cup Winners' Cup, UEFA Cup and two UEFA Super Cups. Oh, and don't forget the record 33 Eredivisie titles up to 2013 and 18 Dutch Cups between 1917 and 2010. Ajax are trophy-tastic!

GAME PLAN

Ever since the 1960s and '70s when Ajax became a huge footy force, the team has played in an attacking and passing style. In 2017-18 they were managed by Marcel Keizer and Eric ten Hag, using a style where they tried to keep the ball and pick holes in the opposition defence. The phrase 'Total Football' came from legendary coach Rinus Michels. who made Ajax such an entertaining and successful passing team in the '60s and '70s.

STARS TO WATCH...

HAKIM ZIYECH
MIDFIELDER
Epic No.10 playmaker

MATTHIJS DE LIGT
DEFENDER
Reliable & great tackler

ANDRE ONANA
GOALKEEPER
Top ex-Barcelona stopper

KLAAS-JAN HUNTELAAR
STRIKER
Experienced goal machine

NICKNAME: Godenzonen
STADIUM: Johan Cruyff ArenA
CAPACITY: 54,033
HOME KIT: Red and white
YEAR FOUNDED: 1900
CLUB LEGENDS: Johan Cruyff, Rinus Michels, Frank de Boer, Marco Van Basten, Patrick Kluivert

JUSTIN KLUIVERT

Striker **Justin Kluivert** is the son of Patrick Kluivert, who scored for Ajax in the 1995 Champions League final.

Justin turned **19** in May **2018**. He played his first game for Ajax aged **17**.

His father scored an impressive **40** goals in **79** games for Holland.

He can play as a **left winger** or as a **support striker**.

In November **2017** Justin scored his first **hat-trick** for Ajax.

Kluivert received his first call-up to the senior **Holland** squad in March **2018**.

The teenager was part of the Ajax squad that lost the **2017** Europa League final against Manchester United.

CAPTAIN: Joel Veltman **TOP SCORER:** Piet van Reenen (273) **YOUNG STAR:** Justin Kluivert

PSV EINDHOVEN

With a proud history and rows of trophies in the cabinet, PSV are a Dutch club with plenty of glamour, glitz and great goalscorers.

SUPER STRIKERS

Check out these awesome goal scorers who've busted nets for PSV Eindhoven! As well as brilliant Brazilians like Romario and Ronaldo, former Manchester United ace Ruud Van Nistelrooy struck 60 league goals in just two seasons. Mateja Kezman, Jan Vennegoor of Hesselink, Jefferson Farfan, Memphis Depay and the legendary Dutchman Ruud Gullit have all top scored for the club since 1986.

TROPHY TALK

PSV fans have enjoyed lots of title parties in the 21st century, with eight Eredivisie crowns between 2001 and 2016. The club have had 23 victories since their first in 1929 and up to 2016. Like Dutch rivals Ajax, PSV also boast top European trophies. They captured the European Cup in 1988 and the UEFA Cup ten years earlier.

STARS TO WATCH...

HIRVING LOZANO
WINGER
Skilful & direct

DANIEL SCHWAAB
DEFENDER
Great positional play

STEVEN BERGWIJN
WINGER
Loves battling defenders

MARKO VAN GINKEL
MIDFIELDER
Ace passing & scoring

NICKNAME: The Lightbulbs
STADIUM: Philips Stadion
CAPACITY: 35,000
HOME KIT: Red and white
YEAR FOUNDED: 1913
CLUB LEGENDS: Guus Hiddink, Romario, Coen Dillen, Ronaldo, Luc Nilis

PLAYER POWER

Thanks to a great group of players and strong teamwork, PSV lost just three of their first 27 Eredivisie games in 2017-18. Hirving Lozano, Luuk de Jong and Marco van Ginkel all reached double figures in goals. Lozano, a versatile and speedy Mexican winger, made seven assists in his first 22 games last season. Steven Bergwijn is another winger lighting up the Philips Stadium and attracting interest from big clubs in England and Spain.

MANAGER: Phillip Cocu **TOP LEAGUE SCORER:** Willy van der Kuijlen (308) **YOUNG STAR:** Mauro Junior

ALL ABOUT FEYENOORD

It's time to rock up in Rotterdam to reveal all the footy figures and facts about the top Dutch team Feyenoord!

VAN THE MAN

Since Giovanni Van Bronckhorst became Feyenoord manager in 2015, he won the Dutch Cup in 2016 and the league in 2017. As a former Feyenoord and Holland captain, Van Bronckhorst has shot the club back into the big time and pulled off wins against Manchester United and Napoli in Europe. The coach likes to play a 4-4-2 formation, built around the attacking talent of Steven Berghuis.

TROPHY TALK

In 2017, Feyenoord ended an 18-year wait to be Dutch champions for the 15th time. On the last day of the season, their 3-1 win over Heracles meant they took the title, beating Ajax by just one point. Feyenoord were fearsome in the 1960s and '70s, winning six leagues and the European and UEFA Cup. They also lifted the UEFA Cup in 2002 and have 12 Dutch Cups between 1930 and 2016.

STARS TO WATCH...

KARIM EL AHMADI
MIDFIELDER
Defends & attacks

BRAD JONES
GOALKEEPER
Super-experienced stopper

TONNY VILHENA
MIDFIELDER
Driving runs & energy

ROBIN VAN PERSIE
STRIKER
Lethal left foot

NICKNAME: The Stadium Club
STADIUM: De Kuip
CAPACITY: 51,177
HOME KIT: Red and white
YEAR FOUNDED: 1908
CLUB LEGENDS: Dirk Kuyt

PLAYER POWER

Former Watford player Berghuis is the star of the show at De Kuip. In his first 27 league games last season, the wonder winger clocked up 12 goals and nine assists. He can play across the midfield, but usually dazzles down the right and cuts in on his left. Jens Toornstra and Tonny Vilhena deliver goals from midfield too, with Denmark's Nicolai Jorgensen leading Feyenoord's strikeforce. Robin Van Persie rejoined the club in January 2018.

CAPTAIN: Karim El Ahmadi **TOP LEAGUE SCORER:** Coen Moulijn (171) **YOUNG STAR:** Dylan Vente

CHANGING ROOM CHANGES

ADO DEN HAAG

Can you spot five changes between each of these Dutch teams' changing room pictures?

ADO DEN HAAG					PSV EINDHOVEN				
1	2	3	4	5	1	2	3	4	5

PSV EINDHOVEN

ANSWERS ON PAGE 94.

BEST OF THE REST!

Here's a super-quick study of six slick European footy leagues. Boost your knowledge with these winners and top players...

Of course I'm in a hurry – I'm Russian!

Krasnodar striker **Fyodor Smolov** was the Russian Premier League top scorer in **2017** and **2016**.

RUSSIA

PREMIER LEAGUE

MAIN CLUBS: Lokomotiv Moscow, Spartak Moscow, CSKA Moscow, Rubin Kazan, Zenit St Petersburg

The mighty Moscow clubs have dominated the Russian Premier League in recent years, but Zenit took the title in 2015. Strikers like Fyodor Smolov (Krasnodar) and Hulk (Zenit) have been top scorers in the league.

BELGIUM

PRO LEAGUE

MAIN CLUBS: Anderlecht, Club Brugge, Standard Liege, KAA Gent

Anderlecht won Belgium's top league five times between 2010 and 2017, with KAA Gent and Brugge the only other teams with titles this decade. In the Champions League last season, Anderlecht won once, with a 1-0 win over Celtic.

AUSTRIA

BUNDESLIGA

MAIN CLUBS: Red Bull Salzburg, Rapid Vienna, Sturm Graz

Red Bull Salzburg have stormed away with the Austrian title lately, picking up every one since 2014. Manus Dabbur fired in the goals for them last season. Rapid Vienna are top dogs overall though in Austria, with their 32nd championship in 2008.

GREECE

SUPERLEAGUE

MAIN CLUBS: Olympiakos, Panathinaikos, AEK Athens

Olympiakos totally boss the Greek Superleague, collecting seven championships in a row between 2011 and 2017. Panathinaikos have 17 league trophies, with the latest in 2010, and AEK Athens came second in 2017.

SWITZERLAND

SUPER LEAGUE

MAIN CLUBS: FC Basel, Young Boys, FC Zurich

In 2018, Young Boys finally stopped Basel's brilliant run of eight Super League crowns in a row. It was their first championship since 1986, but at least Basel had a brilliant 2-1 win at Manchester City in March to celebrate!

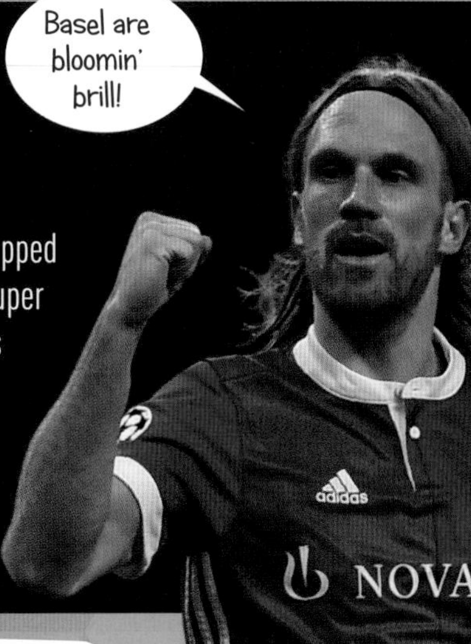

TURKEY

SUPER LIG

MAIN CLUBS: Galatasaray, Besiktas, Istanbul Basaksehir, Fenerbahce

There's a fierce rivalry between the big Istanbul clubs in the Turkish Super Lig! Besiktas topped the league in 2017 and 2016, with Galatasaray the champs in 2012, 2013 and 2015. Fenerbahce were the winners in 2011 and 2014.

ALL ABOUT

MAJOR LEAGUE SOCCER

Outside of the European action, the USA and Canada have some awesome teams competing for trophies and glory. Check out all the facts and stats.

Major League Soccer (MLS) was set up in America and Canada in 1993. In 2018 there are 23 teams competing to lift the MLS Cup, which is the trophy awarded to the team that wins the play-offs and becomes league champions. Toronto FC, Seattle Sounders, Portland Timbers, Los Angeles Galaxy and Sporting Kansas City have all lifted the silverware in recent years.

Ear we go,
ear we go,
ear we go!

There's also a big rivalry in New York, between the Red Bulls and New York City FC. NYCFC are managed by ex-Arsenal legend Patrick Vieira and have Spain's World Cup winner David Villa up front. For New York Red Bulls, Bradley Wright-Phillips hit 87 goals in 140 MLS appearances and picked up the Golden Boot award in 2014 and 2016.

Under coach Greg Vanney, Toronto FC had an amazing season in 2017! With Jozy Altidore, Sebastian Giovinco and Victor Vazquez scoring and creating goals, Toronto won the treble of MLS Cup, Supporters' Shield and Canadian Championship. It was The Reds' best-ever season and the fans went crazy!

MLS CUP CHAMPIONS

2017	Toronto FC
2016	Seattle Sounders
2015	Portland Timbers
2014	LA Galaxy
2013	Sporting Kansas City
2012	LA Galaxy
2011	LA Galaxy
2010	Colorado Rapids

Before Toronto's triumph, Los Angeles Galaxy were the last team to claim the Supporters' Shield and MLS Cup in the same season back in 2011. LA Galaxy have had lots of star players over the last ten years, including David Beckham, Steven Gerrard and Robbie Keane. The club now has a city rivalry with Los Angeles FC, which began competing in the MLS in 2018. LAFC have former Arsenal and Real Sociedad forward Carlos Vela in their strike force.

STARS TO WATCH...

GIOVANI DOS SANTOS
FORWARD
LA GALAXY
Skilful ex-Barcelona ace

EZEQUIEL BARCO
MIDFIELDER
ATLANTA UNITED
Versatile attacking star

JESUS MEDINA
MIDFIELDER
NEW YORK CITY FC
Exciting young goal threat

LAURENT CIMAN
DEFENDER
LOS ANGELES FC
Powerful tackling

ALL ABOUT

BRAZILIAN SERIE A

Brazilian clubs, players and style of play are some of the best on the planet! Jump into this footy-mad land to discover more about their league...

Brazil is the most famous international and World Cup team, so the Brazilian top flight league must be pretty epic too! Called the Campeonato Serie A, it has 20 teams and the big boys of Corinthians, Palmeiras, Santos, Sao Paulo, Cruzeiro and Fluminese scrap it out for the trophy each year. The season lasts from May to December. It's full of goals, skills, exciting young stars and passionate fans!

Corinthians have enjoyed the most success this decade with league titles in 2011, 2015 and 2017. In 2016, Palmeiras won a record 9th championship and were runners-up in 2017. Fluminense's Henrique Dourado and Corinthians' Jo were the league's top scorers that season, with Dourado now a Flamengo star and Jo playing in Japan's J-League.

Teams that finish in the top eight of Serie A can qualify for the Copa Libertadores. This is the most famous club competition in South America, a bit like the Champions League, with top clubs from Argentina, Uruguay, Paraguay and Colombia taking part. In 2017, Brazil's Gremio were Copa Libertadores champions for the third time after beating Lanus from Argentina.

CLUBS WITH FOUR OR MORE TITLES

Palmeiras	Flamengo
Santos	Cruzeiro
Corinthians	Vasco
Sao Paulo	Fluminese

Gustavo Scarpa is a creative attacking player to keep an eye on in Serie A. The Brazilian was the league's top goal creator in 2017 with 12 assists for Fluminese. He joined rivals Palmeiras the following season. Current Watford forward Richarlison is another former Fluminese ace and Gabriel Jesus, now with Manchester City, used to star for Palmeiras in Brazil.

STARS TO WATCH...

GABRIEL BARBOSA
SANTOS
STRIKER
Fearsome in the box

FRED
CRUZEIRO
STRIKER
Awesome goal poacher

LUAN VIEIRA
GREMIO
MIDFIELDER
Cool attacking talent

FELIPE MELO
PALMEIRAS
MIDFIELDER
Super strength & tackling

ALL ABOUT

ARGENTINE SUPERLIGA

Do you fancy knowing a bit more about Argentina's top competition and its biggest clubs? No worries, you've come to just the perfect place!

Argentina's Superliga is stuffed with famous football clubs, including Boca Juniors, Independiente, River Plate, Racing Club, Newell's Old Boys and Argentinos Juniors. In recent years, no team has really dominated the competition with Boca, Lanus, River Plate and Velez Sarsfield all tasting success. Just like in Brazil, the top teams can qualify for the Copa Libertadores.

It's Tevez time, baby! Oh yeah.

In 2014, River Plate, from Buenos Aires, lifted a record 36th title. Boca's triumph in 2017 was their 32nd overall and the two clubs have a mega rivalry, with matches between them called the Superclasico. Boca's most dangerous striker, Carlos Tevez, scored an unforgettable double in the Superclasico in 2016 as Boca won 4-2 at River Plate.

Independiente, from the city of Avellaneda, haven't enjoyed league success since their 2002 Apertura victory. This is the title given to the league's top team at the halfway point of the season. But, the club proudly boasts the most overall titles in the Copa Libertadores. Independiente have seven, coming in 1984, 1975, 1974, 1973, 1972, 1965 and 1964. That's more than bigger South American teams like Sao Paulo and Santos.

Martin Palermo retired in 2011 as Boca Juniors' all-time top scorer. The Argentina ace struck 236 goals between 1997 and 2001 and 2004 to 2011. In total the powerful predator bagged 306 in his career, which also included spells with Alaves, Real Betis and Villarreal in Spain. Palermo's a hero at Boca with six titles and two Copa Libertadores.

STARS TO WATCH...

LUCAS GAMBA
UNION SANTA FE
FORWARD
Great scorer & creator

DARIO BENEDETTO
BOCA JUNIORS
STRIKER
Fab finisher, back from injury

LAUTARO MARTINEZ
RACING CLUB
STRIKER
Tricky young goal-getter

IGNACIO SCOCCO
RIVER PLATE
STRIKER
Great touch & skill

ALL ABOUT CLUB WORLD CUP

Real Madrid's Cristiano Ronaldo scored a hat-trick in the 4-2 final victory over Kashima Antlers in 2016. Ronaldo also netted the winner in the 2017 final against Gremio.

FIFA's Club World Cup is held every year between some of the world's biggest teams. Discover more mega facts about this incredible event!

The **Club World Cup** is a knockout competition between the winners of the Champions League in Europe, Asia, Africa, North America and Oceania. The Copa Libertadores winners and the host country's champions also take part.

Real Madrid won the Club World Cup for a third time in **2017**. They also became the first team to win it two years in a row, after their success in **2016**.

Barcelona also picked up their third trophy in **2015**. Lionel Messi and the lads took the title in **2011** and **2009**.

In **2008**, **Manchester United** became the first British club to win the Club World Cup. The Red Devils beat Ecuador's LDU Quito 1-0 in the final.

In **2005**, **Liverpool** lost the Club World Cup final 1-0 to Brazil's Sao Paulo. Chelsea also lost the 2012 final to Corinthians.

The first competition was in **2000**. Corinthians, from Brazil, were the champions.

In **2017**, New Zealand's **Auckland City Football Club** played in the tournament for a record ninth time.

COOL KIDS

Have a go at guessing who these footy superstars are, from these pictures of when they were youngsters!

ANSWER ....

ANSWER ....

ANSWER ....

ANSWER ....

ANSWER ....

ANSWER ....

ANSWER ....

ANSWER ....

ANSWER ....

ANSWERS ON PAGE 94.

PICK YOUR WORLD DREAM TEAM!

You've seen the most awesome and epic players on the planet. Now it's your turn to be the boss and pick your ultimate world footy Dream Team!

GOALKEEPER

Your fantasy team will need a top stopper with mega reflexes and perfect kicking, catching and passing. Who will you go for?

- Manuel Neuer, Bayern Munich ☐
- Gianluigi Buffon, Juventus ☐
- Keylor Navas, Real Madrid ☐
- Jan Oblak, Atletico Madrid ☐
- Marc-Andre ter Stegen, Barcelona ☐
- Iker Casillas, Porto ☐
- Samir Handanovic, Inter Milan ☐
- Alisson, Roma ☐
- Roman Burki, Borussia Dortmund ☐
- Christian Puggioni, Sampdoria ☐

Other: ________

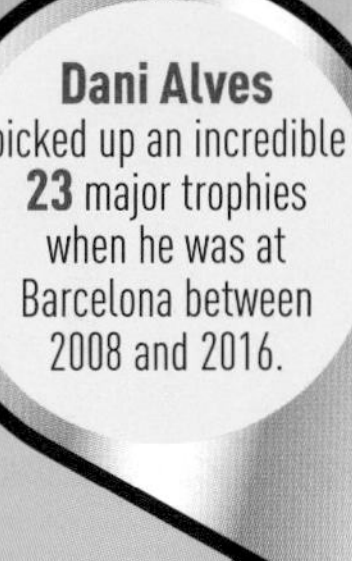

RIGHT-BACK

This position needs an awesome athlete who can defend and attack and also has never-ending energy to cover the pitch!

- Dani Alves, PSG ☐
- Joshua Kimmich, Bayern Munich ☐
- Dani Carvajal, Real Madrid ☐
- Sergi Roberto, Barcelona ☐
- Mattia De Sciglio, Juventus ☐
- Djibril Sidibe, Monaco ☐
- Ricardo Pereira, Porto ☐
- Thomas Meunier, PSG ☐
- Elseid Hysaj, Napoli ☐
- Joao Cancelo, Inter Milan ☐

Other: ____________

LEFT-BACK

A lethal left foot that can cross the ball, ping passes and make great tackles is top of your wish list! Time to take your pick...

- Faouzi Ghoulam, Napoli ☐
- Alex Sandro, Juventus ☐
- Filipe Luis, Atletico Madrid ☐
- David Alaba, Bayern Munich ☐
- Jordi Alba, Barcelona ☐
- Marcelo, Real Madrid ☐
- Layvin Kurzawa, PSG ☐
- Raphael Guerreiro, Borussia Dortmund ☐
- Ricardo Rodriguez, AC Milan ☐
- Jonas Hector, Cologne ☐

Other: ____________

BE THE BOSS

CENTRE-BACK

Selecting two centre-backs from this list of quality defenders won't be easy! Which pair of players will make your dream team?

- Dayot Upamecano, RB Leipzig ☐
- Gerard Pique, Barcelona ☐
- Diego Godin, Atletico Madrid ☐
- Leonardo Bonucci, AC Milan ☐
- Thiago Silva, PSG ☐
- Sergio Ramos, Real Madrid ☐
- Raphael Varane, Real Madrid ☐
- Mats Hummels, Bayern Munich ☐
- Kalidou Koulibaly, Napoli ☐
- Raul Albiol, Napoli ☐
- Giorgio Chiellini, Juventus ☐

Other: ____________

MIDFIELDER

Take your time to get the right balance from your three central midfielders. Speed, power, skills, and defending are the key things.

- Andres Iniesta, Barcelona ☐
- Ivan Rakitic, Barcelona ☐
- Luka Modric, Real Madrid ☐
- Marco Asensio, Real Madrid ☐
- Isco, Real Madrid ☐
- Angel Di Maria, PSG ☐
- Florian Thauvin, Marseille ☐
- Donny van de Beek, Ajax ☐
- Fabinho, Monaco ☐
- Marek Hamsik, Napoli ☐
- Arturo Vidal, Bayern Munich ☐

Other: ____________

MY DREAM TEAM LINE-UP IS...

STRIKER

This is the most exciting thing about being a dream team boss – choosing the three fantastic forwards to lead your strike force!

- Paulo Dybala, Juventus ☐
- Neymar, PSG ☐
- Edinson Cavani, PSG ☐
- Cristiano Ronaldo, Real Madrid ☐
- Lionel Messi, Barcelona ☐
- Luis Suarez, Barcelona ☐
- Robert Lewandowski, Bayern Munich ☐
- Antoine Griezmann, Atletico Madrid ☐
- Jonas, Benfica ☐
- Justin Kluivert, Ajax ☐
- Radamel Falcao, Monaco ☐

Other: ____________

Paulo Dybala scored against Tottenham in **2018** to knock them out of the Champions League.

PAULO DYBALA

These superhero stars have footy skills that are from another planet! Discover some of the best female talent in the world...

WONDER WOMEN!

MARTA

MAIN CLUBS: Orlando Pride, FC Rosengard, Umea IK
COUNTRY: Brazil

- Legendary striker with 5 World Player of the Year awards
- Speedy, Skilful and loves to dribble
- 15 goals in 17 World Cup finals games

ADA HEGERBERG

MAIN CLUBS: Lyon, Turbine Potsdam
COUNTRY: Norway

- Talented young striker with deadly accurate shooting skills
- Won the league, cup and Champions League treble with Lyon
- Winner of the UEFA Best Women's Player in Europe award in 2016

CARLI LLOYD

MAIN CLUBS: Sky Blue FC, Western New York Flash, Houston Dash
COUNTRY: USA

- FA Women's Cup winner with Manchester City in 2017
- Women's World Cup champion and Golden Ball trophy
- Incredible scoring record with 98 in 247 games for USA

LUCY BRONZE

MAIN CLUBS: Lyon, Manchester City, Liverpool LFC
COUNTRY: England

- Tough right-back with a cool head and top skills
- Moved to Lyon in France in 2017
- Named in the all-star FIFPro Women's World XI team

LIEKE MARTENS

MAIN CLUBS: Barcelona, Rosengard, Standard Liege
COUNTRY: Netherlands

- 2017 Best FIFA Women's Player and UEFA Player of the Year
- Goal scoring left winger with magic skills
- UEFA Women's EURO 2017 winner and Player of the Tournament

ANDRINE HEGERBERG

MAIN CLUBS: PSG, Birmingham City
COUNTRY: Norway

- Stylish and energetic midfielder
- Starred for Birmingham in the WSL
- Older sister, and Norwegian team mate, to Ada Hegerberg

ALEX MORGAN

MAIN CLUBS: Lyon, Orland Pride, Portland Thorns FC
COUNTRY: USA

- Awesome goal scorer for club and country
- Over 80 strikes for USA since 2010
- World Cup and Olympic gold winner

ANSWERS

Page 16-17 Lookin' For legends!

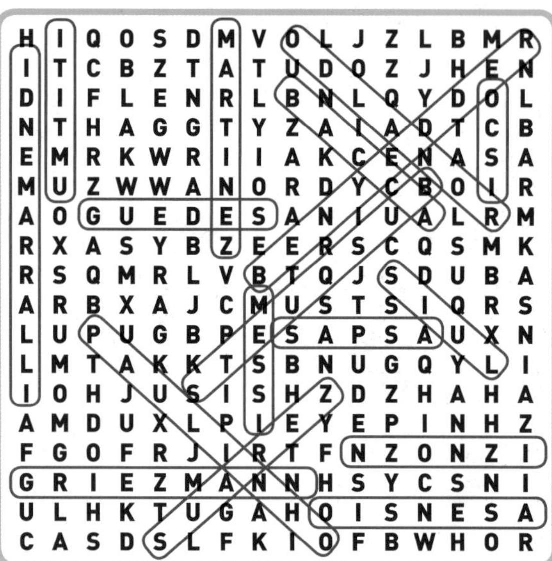

Pages 26-27 Name Game

1. Bayer Leverkusen, 2. Werder Bremen, 3. Eintracht Frankfurt, 4. Hertha Berlin, 5. Wolfsburg

Pages 32-33 Face the Facts!

1. Kylian Mbappe (PSG), 2. Philippe Coutinho (Barcelona), 3. Arjen Robben (Bayern Munich), 4. Luke Modric (Real Madrid), 5. Gianluigi Buffon (Juventus), 6. Christian Pulisic (Borussia Dortmund), 7. Neymar (PSG), 8. Sergio Ramos (Real Madrid)

Pages 42-43 Hit or Miss?

1. Goal, 2. Goal, 3. No goal, 4. No goal, 5. Goal

Pages 52-53 Ligue 1 Lads!

PREMIER PICKS: 1. Rafael Da Silva (Lyon), 2. Angel Di Maria (PSG), 3. Diafra Sakho (West Ham United).
CLOSE CALL: Zlatan Ibrahimovic, Paris Saint-Germain.
PAYING THE PENALTY: Ball No. 4. GUESS THE YEAR: 1. 2013, 2. 2008, 3. 2016

Pages 66-67 Head to Toe

1. J, 2. C, 3. A, 4. H, 5. B, 6. L, 7. K, 8. D, 9. F. 10, E. 11, G. 12, I

Pages 74-75 Changing Room Changes

ADO DEN HAAG

PSV EINDHOVEN

Page 86 Cool Kids

1. Luis Suarez (Barcelona, pictured with Groningen); 2. Neymar (PSG, pictured with Santos); 3. Arjen Robben (Bayern Munich, pictured with PSV); 4. Gerard Pique (Barcelona, pictured with Manchester United); 5. Edinson Cavani (PSG, pictured with Palermo); 6. Thomas Muller (Bayern Munich); 7. Sergio Ramos (Real Madrid, pictured with Sevilla); 8. Antoine Griezmann